GPS TECHNOLOGY

by Tammy Gagne

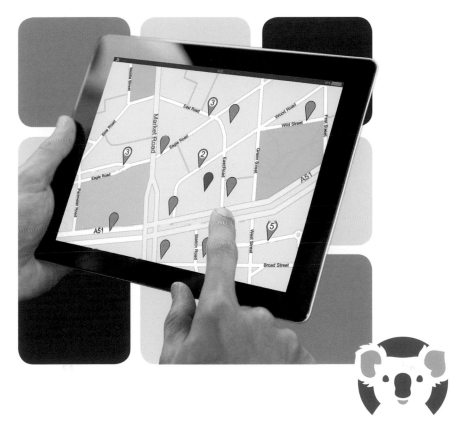

Cody Koala

An Imprint of Pop!
popbooksonline.com

abdopublishing.com
Published by Pop!, a division of ABDO, PO Box 398166, Minneapolis, Minnesota 55439. Copyright © 2019 by POP, LLC. International copyrights reserved in all countries. No part of this book may be reproduced in any form without written permission from the publisher. Pop!™ is a trademark and logo of POP, LLC.

Printed in the United States of America, North Mankato, Minnesota

042018
092018

THIS BOOK CONTAINS RECYCLED MATERIALS

Cover Photo: Shutterstock Images
Interior Photos: Shutterstock Images, 1, 6 (bottom right), 6 (top right), 9 (bottom right), 16–17; MSFC/NASA, 5; iStockphoto, 6 (bottom left), 9 (top), 9 (bottom left), 10, 13; Charles D. Gaddis IV/US Navy, 15; Elaine Thompson/AP Images, 19; Jamie Gates/American Press/AP Images, 20

Editor: Charly Haley
Series Designer: Laura Mitchell

Library of Congress Control Number: 2017963464
Publisher's Cataloging-in-Publication Data
Names: Gagne, Tammy, author.
Title: GPS technology / by Tammy Gagne.
Other title: Global Positioning System technology
Description: Minneapolis, Minnesota : Pop!, 2019. | Series: 21st century inventions | Includes online resources and index.
Identifiers: ISBN 9781532160417 (lib.bdg.) | ISBN 9781532161537 (ebook) |
Subjects: LCSH: Global Positioning System--Juvenile literature. | Technological innovations--Juvenile literature. | Inventions--History--Juvenile literature. | Technology--History--Juvenile literature.
Classification: DDC 609--dc23

Cody Koala

Pop open this book and you'll find QR codes like this one, loaded with information, so you can learn even more!

Scan this code* and others like it while you read, or visit the website below to make this book pop.

popbooksonline.com/gps-technology

*Scanning QR codes requires a web-enabled smart device with a QR code reader app and a camera.

Table of Contents

Chapter 1

What Is GPS?

GPS stands for global positioning system. The system is made up of **satellites** in space. The satellites send information to GPS **devices** on Earth.

Watch a video here!

GPS satellites in space track locations on Earth. They send that information to GPS devices on Earth. This shows people where things are.

People use these devices to know where they are. GPS devices are built into some cars and smartphones.

Chapter 2

How We Use GPS

Many people use GPS devices to get from one place to another.

Even airplanes and ships use GPS.

Learn more here!

People tell their GPS device where they want to go. Then the GPS tracks their location and gives them directions on the way. Most devices will say the directions out loud.

GPS **technology** became more available to people in the 2000s. Before then, most people used paper maps to find their way.

Mapping Our World

Scientists, the government, the military, and companies use GPS to create many different maps.

Learn more here!

A construction company

might use GPS to **survey**

land that it wants to build on.

An oil company might survey
land where it wants to drill.

More Ways to Use GPS

GPS is used for much more than directions and mapping. Scientists use GPS to track wild animals. This helps them learn more about those animals.

GPS tracking collar

Complete an activity here!

Scientists use GPS to study the weather. They can find wind speeds by tracking objects such as balloons.

GPS technology is still changing. People will use GPS for even more things in the future.

Making Connections

Text-to-Self

Have you or your parents used GPS to get from one place to another?

Text-to-Text

Have you read another book about GPS or other modern technology? What did you learn in that book?

Text-to-World

Do you think GPS is useful to the world as a whole? Why or why not?

Glossary

device – an object made for a specific purpose.

satellite – a human-made object that moves in space around Earth for science.

survey – examining something by taking measurements.

technology – objects created by using science.

Index

Online Resources

popbooksonline.com

Thanks for reading this Cody Koala book!

Scan this code* and others like it in this book, or visit the website below to make this book pop!

popbooksonline.com/gps-technology

*Scanning QR codes requires a web-enabled smart device with a QR code reader app and a camera.

3972